ALL SHOOK UP

Books available by Adrian Mitchell

POETRY

Love Songs of World War Three (Allison & Busby/W.H. Allen, 1989)
Greatest Hits: His 40 Golden Greats (Bloodaxe Books, 1991)
Blue Coffee: Poems 1985-1996 (Bloodaxe Books, 1996)
Heart on the Left: Poems 1953-1984 (Bloodaxe Books, 1997)
All Shook Up: Poems 1997-2000 (Bloodaxe Books, 2000)

PLAYS

The Pied Piper (Oberon Books)
Gogol: The Government Inspector (Methuen)
Calderón: The Mayor of Zalamea & two other plays (Absolute Classics)
Lope de Vega: Fuente Ovejuna and Lost in a Mirror (Absolute Classics)
Tyger Two, Man Friday, Satie Day/Night and *In the Unlikely Event
  of an Emergency* (Oberon Books)
The Siege (Oberon Books)
The Snow Queen (Oberon Books)
The Mammoth Sails Tonight! (Oberon Books)
The Lion, the Witch and the Wardrobe (Oberon Books)

POETRY FOR CHILDREN

The Orchard Book of Poems (Orchard, 1993)
The Thirteen Secrets of Poetry (Macdonald, 1993)
Balloon Lagoon (Orchard, 1997)
Dancing in the Street (Orchard, 1999)

CHILDREN'S STORIES

The Ugly Duckling (Dorling Kindersley)
The Steadfast Tin Soldier (Dorling Kindersley)
Maudie and the Green Children (Tradewind)
Nobody Rides the Unicorn (Transworld)
My Cat Mrs Christmas (Orion)
The Adventures of Robin Hood and Marian (Orchard Books)

RECORDINGS

The Dogfather (57 Productions – double CD)

ALL SHOOK UP

POEMS 1997-2000

BLOODAXE BOOKS

ISBN: 1 85224 513 1

First published 2000 by
Bloodaxe Books Ltd,
Highgreen,
Tarset,
Northumberland NE48 1RP.

Bloodaxe Books Ltd acknowledges
the financial assistance of Northern Arts.

Cover printing by J. Thomson Colour Printers Ltd, Glasgow.

Printed in Great Britain by
Cromwell Press Ltd, Trowbridge, Wiltshire.

To my beloved Celia

and to my children
Alistair, Danny, Briony, Sasha and Beattie

and to my grandchildren
Natasha, Charlotte, Caitlin, Zoe, Arthur, Lola and Robin

with love always

ACKNOWLEDGEMENTS

Poems in *All Shook Up* have previously appeared in *Peace News, Raw Edge, The Independent* and the *New Statesman*, and have been broadcast on the BBC's *Poetry Please.*

Song lyrics have appeared in the texts of the plays *The Mammoth Sails Tonight!* and *The Snow Queen,* both published by Oberon Books.

Much of my poetry these days goes into plays with songs (for children and adults) and books (for children). That's fine with me. I like the Lone Ranger kick of riding into a new town to perform my poems, but I also like forming or joining a theatre gang and working as part of a team.

The lyrics in the *Showsongs* section come from two different shows. 'Shake My Soul', 'Four Windows', 'Orpheus Sings' and 'Music' are all from *Orpheus Sings,* one of the plays for young people which forms the Greek myth trilogy *The Heroes.* (The other two plays are *The Gorgon's Head* and *The Maze of the Minotaur.*) These were commissioned by the Kageboushi Young People's Theatre in Japan and then translated. They opened in a circus tent in the centre of Tokyo and then toured Japan. Music by Andrew Dickson.

'Start Again' is a choral song cycle written to celebrate the 50th anniversary of the Universal Declaration of Human Rights, commissioned by the Arts Council of England and organised in support of Amnesty. Music is by Peter Moser, whose energy and inspiration made an impossible project work in many towns and cities.

EDUCATIONAL NOTE TO ALL WOODHEADS

None of the work in this or any of my other books is to be used in connection with any examination whatsoever. I'm happy if people who like them choose to learn them, recite them or sing them in schools. But please don't make anyone study them or write essays about them. Why? Because examinations were a social experiment which has failed dismally. And because there are too many pointless essays in the world already.

CONTENTS

Sublime and Ridiculous Introductions

The book opens with 'Power and Gentleness' – a poem or part of a poem I found recently in one of William Hone's marvellous anthologies – *The Year Book*. I don't know who wrote these lines but they speak for me and conjure up the work of that genius, my friend and sometime collaborator Ralph Steadman.

Peace.

Power and Gentleness

I've thought, in gentle and ungentle hour,
Of many an act and giant shape of power;
Of the old kings with high exacting looks,
Sceptred and globed; of eagles on their rocks
With straining feet, and that fierce mouth and drear,
Answering the strain with downward drag austere;
Of the rich-headed lion, whose huge frown,
All his great nature, gathering, seems to crown;
Then of cathedral, with its priestly height,
Seen from below at superstitious sight;
Of ghastly castle, that eternally
Holds its blind visage out to the lone sea;
And of all sunless subterranean deeps
The creature makes, who listens while he sleeps,
Avarice; and then of those old earthly cones
That stride, they say, over heroic bones;
And those stone heaps Egyptian, whose small doors
Look like low dens under precipitous shores;
And him great Memnon, that long sitting by
In seeming idleness, with stony eye,
Sang at the morning's touch, like poetry;
And then of all the fierce and bitter fruit
Of the proud planting of a tyrannous foot; –
Of bruised rights, and flourishing bad men;
And virtue wasting heav'nwards from a den;
Brute force and fury; and the devilish drouth
Of the fool cannon's ever-gaping mouth;
And the bride-widowing sword; and the harsh bray
The sneering trumpet sends across the fray;
And all which lights the people-thinning star
That selfishness invokes, – the horsed war
Panting along with many a bloody mane.

I've thought of all this pride and all this pain,
And all the insolent plenitudes of power,
And I declare, by this most quiet hour,
Which holds, in different tasks, by the fire-light,
Me and my friends here this delightful night,
That Power itself has not one half the might
Of Gentleness. 'Tis want to all true wealth,
The uneasy madman's force to the wise health;
Blind downward beating, to the eyes that see;
Noise to persuasion, doubt to certainty;

The consciousness of strength in enemies,
Who must be strained upon, or else they rise,
The battle to the moon, who all the while,
High out of hearing passes with her smile;
The Tempest, trampling in his scanty run,
To the whole globe, that basks about the sun;
Or as all shrieks and clangs, with which a sphere,
Undone and fired, could rake the midnight ear,
Compared with that vast dumbness nature keeps
Throughout her million starried deeps,
Most old, and mild, and awful, and unbroken,
Which tells a tale of peace, beyond whate'er was spoken.

(from the *Literary Pocket Book*, 1819,
quoted by William Hone in his *Year Book*)

Introduction – For Lovers Only

Now if you want your woman
To understand
Just take this little book
And place it in her hand

It may take a line
It may take a page
But she'll jump out at you
Like a lion from a cage

And if you want your man
But he won't take the hint
Just open up the pages
Let him feel the print

Touch his nose with the spine
Stroke his cheek with the cover
Have him sniff the index
And he'll turn into a lover

But if you want to stay together
For more than one chariot ride
You'd better read aloud to each other
Every one of the poems inside.

Whisper them at midnight
Sing them all at dawn
And nine months later
Who knows what'll be born –
Maybe a unicorn?

THE YEARS SPEED BY

A Year Passes, as Years Do

January is a penguin on a slide of ice
on an iceberg full of penguins
watching a film called *Iceberg*
about an iceberg badly damaged by a monster ship
and a love affair between two of the penguins
but only one survived
there is a terrible song in the film
called *Our Fish Will Go On*.

February is a man called Fred
with cardboard in the soles of his holy shoes
as the Manchester rain pours down
and slaps his face with its chilly hands
and his coat is soaked through
so that putting his scarlet-blue
hands into his pockets only
makes them colder and damper.

March is a kite which breaks free of its string
and surfs across the sky over the South Downs
and sees the far coast of France shining
and starts to slide along the air currents over the Channel
dreaming of a happy landing in Paris.

April is a blue-eyed toddler
who staggers into a field of trampolining lambs
and sits in the meadowgrass
snatching at the raggedy white clouds
and singing a song about chocolate biscuits.

May is an orchard bursting with blossoms
where the bad boys have built
a shadowy hut made of old doors
roof and walls camouflaged with slices of turfs
they may smile and you and promise you surprises
but don't go into the shadowy hut
built by the bad boys.

June is a dancer in the centre of the city
as the businesspeople march past in their uniforms
barking into their voodoophones
she is the only one who looks the sun in the face
as she dances her slip-sloppy dance in the fountain
the big fat sweaty happy dancer who loves the sun.

July is an exhausted old retriever
back from a walk on his three good legs
lying on the cool sofa panting with his tongue
as his eyes flitter shut and the dreams begin
of galloping after rabbits down a mountain of bones
as he sleeps in the arms of his master.

August is a couple of pale crabs under a green rock
complaining about the aliens
with their thudding music and howling voices
and terrible spades wrecking the sandy lands
and emptying pools and generally
upsetting the slow and sideways world
of a couple of old curmudgeons with claws.

September is an apple
in the shaking hands of a young woman
on a bench in the grass compound
behind the mental hospital.
She is afraid to eat the apple.
She is afraid to put the apple down.
Because the apple is her mind.
Because the apple is her heart.
Because the apple is her life.
Because the apple is the world.
She cannot remember the word for apple.

October is a wood of scarlet and gold
and an old poet smiling to himself
as he shuffles through squashy leaves
remembering only the good days gone by
remembering beloved people animals and books
and chuckling inside himself to see
a party of schoolchildren with clipboards and a teacher
who has told them to write poems about October.

November is a bursting bonfire
of souvenirs going up in smoke
a bonfire of grasping high-jumping flames
surrounded by grimy worshippers
as a thousand stars burst in the gunpowdered sky
and down inside the belly of the bonfires
the baked potatoes crackle to each other.

December is a reindeer travelling
across hundreds of miles of golden moss
past the poised pines of dusky forests
over the frosted mirrors of lakes
up down and round about blinding snowscape
to the Snow Queen's Palace
where his friend Gerda sits
with the apple of September in her hands.

Wishing in March

wishing I felt the silver shiver
of the snowberry bush by the whispering river
when the snowberries like starlit treasure
shudder with delicate berrypleasure

Another October

grass is growing greyer daily
thousands of ghosts commuting down the river
muttering crowds of out of work leaves
and the green arias of the trees
join together in a golden chorus

the golden chanting of the woods
echoing between two hills
as the ghosts of lanky sons
and the ghosts of laughing daughters
in coal-black jeans and misty dresses
dance down along the river water
to the drumbeat of the hills

Life Is a Walk Across a Field

(opposite of the Russian proverb, Life is not a walk across a field,
which is the last line of Boris Pasternak's poem 'Hamlet')

Life is a walk across a field
sometimes a golden dreamdrift of polished petals
and daisies bouncing among the hummocks of moss
which guide an infant river sometimes over squashed grass
sometimes under the spongey turf but sometimes

the tickling green surface breaks apart underfoot
and the mouth of the ground gapes
and the bogdragon swallows down your shins
your hips your armpits your chin your –

Life is a walk across a field
and should you find a milkmaid in one hollow
with a jug of cider and breasts like summer
from behind the spectacular oak will steam
the minotaur, half farmer and half bull
guffawing as his horns impale you both oh yes

Life is a walk across the field
of buttercups and landmines…

UNDER NEW LABOUR

That Feeling

When you sit
On a chair
And the chair's
Not there
That's the feeling I mean –
That's the Blair.

We Bomb Tonight
(headline in the *Evening Standard*, London, 17 December 1998)

> *'deafening explosions reverberated across Baghdad last night'*

> *'City traders reacted calmly to the air strikes, with oil prices
> and the dollar retreating after yesterday's sharp gains…'*

me and little sister
sleeping tight
hugged in the arms
of a dark blue night

I was in a funny dream
and both of us
were being driven by a horse
in a dark blue bus

then my dream went bang
night turned day
little sister
was vanished away

and the air was nothing
but dust and screams
now I search for little sister
in all my dreams

she hides I seek
but all I have found
in my dreams is a
dark blue hole in the ground

Education Education Education

Only one reason why I get to school
it's a condition of my parole

chilled a teacher and torched a church
in the cause of criminological research

back to the playground I take my stand
uppers and downers in each hand

if you don't like the deal we made
I'll unzip your kipper with a rusty blade

I'm on the Train

Good good.
Say again?
Sorry. Oh, brilliant!
She's up to speed on that.
Here she is. Bye!!

I'm on Simone's mobile.
Right.
Have you caught up with Matt this morning?
You're a star.
Good.
Sarah got 35 cases of soup
but it's mostly mushroom
so it's up to you what you need for the shoot.
Yes.
Sam's coming up from Saatchi's.
Good good.

The Druggards

The druggards lean in corners of the werehouse
wearing raggerjeans, eight-piece suits,
little block dresses, corrugated overcoats,
   chins like the prows of model yachts
   mouths like slots for credit cards

Brains can be such beautiful islands
but they abandon theirs to the invading
mute and screaming chemical armies
     for they think the brain is only this
     a hunk of electrified meat
     they imagine life is a boredomboardroomboardgame,
     the soul a stamped-out cigarette
     as they cheat each other and trick each other
     and sneer at the undruggard world
     before plotting a petulant suicide...

Hello Humans

Her long honey hair grew so
because a sister grew it so
or a magazine ordered it

the mole perching above the corner of her smile
the way people lean further over the rail
to see the dolphins rising

the vain knocking of waves against
the rocky gates of islands

the soldier who can't afford
more than a tea and doughnut
leans on the vaulted redbrick
customs shed gazing at
the black mirrors of his boots

the tilted heads of sleeping passengers
on the plane home from an exhausting holiday

the pity of it, Iago, the pity of it

they build their nests
in holes under the rocks
they defend their young
against ridiculous odds

they are bitten a thousand times
but never once shy away
from the multitudinous jaws of disaster

how I love the human race
the pity of it

they confidently bark and order
and their theories come marching out of their mouths
like soldiers of an ancient regiment

who parade in the heat of a napalm sun
who parade under fire from uranium-tipped hail
and line up holding up their killer-claws
for the emperor's inspection

they shuffle together
knowing they are undefeatable
this imaginary real army
oh the pity of it

and they plan a tower of babel
for the millennium
with a crèche for all the different species
and an incubator for hatching
the new laid eggs of herons and turtles and cobras
and all the animals who can afford to pay
with uni-species facilities for all
including disabled dandelion clocks
and stones which are too oblong or jagged to roll

oh the pity of it
oh the pit

Go Well

When the last Whale in the whole world
Was hauled through London on an open lorry
One million children trudged behind it
Bearing banners saying Sorry.

Later the last Horse and the last Dog
Rolled by upon their funeral carts.
No children waved Goodbye to them –
All were in hospital with broken hearts.

Shaven Heads

Men in their twenties with shaven heads
Men in their thirties with shaven heads
Men in their forties with shaven heads
They all look alike to me

Their noses jut out like ruddy rockets
Their eyeballs bulge out of their sockets

They smile all the time at people from foreign parts
To show they are not skinhead racist farts

But that smile too frequently unzips
Like a leer and bald heads speak louder than lips

It must feel so weird when you're shaving your crop
Put that razor away grow some sort of a mop

But don't overdo it or I shall wail
Get out of here with your fuzzy pony-tail

John Major's Collected Poem

I love silver –
It brightens
And makes a room smile –
I always think.

Walldream

They collected up, in fine brown nets,
the coal-coloured rocks on the dark side of the moon.

Around the limits of London
in the 28th century
they built a bulging wall of sootrock
a wall with blurred outlines
emitting rays of darkness
so that anyone approaching the city
whether explorer or attacker
became lost in a black fog
and turned, to stagger, blinking, home.

But when the wall builders, time travelling,
visited me last night
They cried out: 'Where are the walls we built?
Where are the Walls of Darkness?'

'Don't worry,' I said, 'Your Walls are in the future
so long as you don't go too far.
Otherwise, you'll find them in the past.'

Hooray Poems

Hooray! Hooray!
I am a merry Pygmy
I sit all day
On a bundle of hay
Playing with my Ombothigme

Hooray! Hooray!
I am a jolly Inuit
It's paradise
To cut a hole in the ice
And shove your neighbour into it

Hooray! Hooray!
I'm a blooming Anglo-Saxon
I hide my terror
In my Ford Sierra
As I bash my fist on the klaxon

At the Dome in the Mirrordrome

O gin ye brak a looking-glass
It's seven years gnarly luck.
Gin ye luke in the glass tae view your ain arse
Ye're one sad fuck.

Change the Subject

Whenever my bottom is dusty
I go to the Bottom Washing Company
And there the Bottom Washing Operative
Washes my bottom with glee

A FEW HAIKU

Haiku About Benevolence

The Good King's palace:
All of its floors are marble –
So kind to the knees.

Yorkshire Haiku
(for Alastair Niven)

Every morning
My grandpa said: 'I'm fed, clothed
And in my right mind.'

Jazz Haiku

The pianist smiles.
His lips are sensuous but
His teeth need tuning.

A Flight of Stairs Haiku

Gliding down was great
Skimming over seven stairs
The snag was landing

Hotel Haiku

briefcase on your bed
packed full with £50 notes
all soaking in blood

Winter Haiku for Emma Chichester-Clark

Two blue moons above
A pair of silver birches –
Emma by snowlight

Oedipus Wrecks the Oedipus Complex Haiku

It isn't complex –
I want to murder mother
And marry father.

Seven Spamku

To: The Pork Luncheon Meat Poetry Festival

Dear Festival,
    *Please accept these Spamku slices as humble entries
in the sizzling pan of your esteemed competition:*

Turner's masterpiece –
Sun And Ocean Colliding
or A Spam Salad?

      My wife quite likes Spam
      My dog Ella quite likes Spam
      Nothing's quite like Spam

Haiku politics –
for the holy name of 'Spam'
please substitute 'Blair'

      Sam ate Spam and burst –
      Spamtaneous combustion
      said the Coroner

Spam goes on and on.
Who but me remembers Spam's
wartime rival, Prem?

    Are Spam chunks floating
    in the sea heavier than
    the Spam-eater's turds?

      This Spamku contest
      has transmogrified my brain
      into solid Spam

THE CARNIVAL OF VENUS

Asymmetrical Love Song

My love is asymmetrical
She looks different from every angle
Some might say she's a little bit wonky
But I say – jingle jangle!

Valances
(with love to Celia)

Today is the first day of my life as a domesticated animal
For I have discovered the meaning of the word valance
Yes and I have handled two different but similar valances
And helped to fit those valances appropriately.

What, you may ask me, is a valance?
Well the centre of the valance
Is a sheet upon which nobody lies.
It is spread on the upper surface of the base of the bed
On which the sun seldom if ever shines
And there the centre of the valance becomes
A sheet for the mattress to repose upon.

I should hazard that even in the suburban world
Inhabited by such underlings as
Doillies, druggets and downtrodden felt,
The valance centre must be numbered with the humblest.
Even were it decorated with a gold-embroidered
Representation of the Signing of the Treaty of Utrecht,
Or hand-sprinkled with a spiders' web
Of luminous paints from Jackson Pollock's fist
Or scorched by the impression of the face of the corpse
Of the great-grandfather of Ian Paisley
It would be unseen and unacclaimed
Except by minions whose duties occasionally oblige them
To change the valances or rearrange the valances.
(So I was not surprised that the two valances
Which I handled today, my two first valances,
Were undecorated in any sense.)

But it is not the centre of the valance
Which is at the heart of valancehood
Any more than it is the underpants of Leonardo da Vinci
Which inspire our admiration.
For all around the centre of the valance runs a margin
And, beyond that margin, a billowing border of linen,
(The same material of which the centre is composed)
But slightly ruched all round.

So, when the mattress is placed upon the valance
The edges of the valance appear all around the waist of the bed
Like a short ballet skirt, a modest tutu,
An edging of wavelets, ready to bear the sleeper
Over a sea of frills and flounces, to the Land of Furbelow.

Celia at Lower Hardacre

gold on the grass or silver snow
up the hollowy track we go

under the tree each daughter stands
big eyes hidden by woolly hands

> *Magic Tree, Magic Tree,*
> *Are there sweeties there for me?*

Polly waves her tail –
this spell can never fail.

Inside the Net

inside that mosquito net
under that cone of gauze
that spotlight of moonlight
we slept like silver fishes in a lake
or an enchanted bride and groom
inside a misty wedding cake

Away

I went out
with open hands
into the strange
and shaking lands

I shake my spear
I shake your hand
I stretch my smile
like a rubber band

is it good to shake
is it good to be shook
come on do the earthquake
and the avalanche book

I could tell you my name
but it's meaningless
like the clothes on the floor
when I undress

call me by any name
you like to say
one name for the night
another for the day

I'm in a far country
and travelling's fun
but tonight it was bad
when you cried on the phone

thousands of miles away
lies my darling
she wears my love
like a silver ring

Arlo Guthrie, Ray Charles, Willie Nelson,
Aretha Franklin and Peggy Lee
they got the voices
say what I long to say

and I wish I could be many species of animal
so I could show how I feel
I'm a stumbling moose
I'm a homeless goose
I'm an unplugged electric eel

love is like a circle
it goes round and round
life is like a spiral
circling down and down

death acts very tough
but he's silly stuff
tries to fill us full of fear
sticks his black iron claw in our ear

lots of my friends have been dragged down there
I'll have to join them eventually
I plan to float down through the glittering blue
to rot proudly in their company

well
that's why I'm shaking
like a six-month pup
on fireworks night
all shook up

The New Baby's First Words

all of us babies are small big heroes

wow!
nine months stuck down in the dark well
a soft small flower
gradually growing eyelid petals
and leafy fingers

seeing nothing beyond the red wall
but hearing
that thumping drumbeat day and night

and finally – the yell!
the writhing and squashing
pushing and squiggling
wild screams
and shoving
squeezing
downwards
through
the tunnel
of muscles

and out into the chilly brightness
and the attack
of
invisible
shocking
icedrink
beautiful air

that's enough adventures for one life surely
time for me to retire from being a hero
I think I'll settle down for good
on this warm and comfortable
milky hill

Wishes to Welcome Two New Babies
(for Zoe and Lola)

the milk of the moon
the wine of the sun
the friendship of grass
and salty sand

adventures with Jumblies
and Peter Rabbit
and all the daft creatures
of Wonderland

Paul, Ringo,
George and John
bless the floors
you dance upon

elephant rides
affectionate apes
and the sheep and rocks
of mountainside farms

a cat which will curl
round your neck like a scarf
and a golden retriever
to lie in your arms

I wish you wild happy and gentle sad
and all the love of your Mum and Dad

Where Are They Now?

My mother lives inside my heart.
I live inside my mother's heart.
My father lives inside my heart.
I live inside my father's heart.

A Lucky Family
(to Helen and Phil)

Their garden's a magical
Welcoming planet
With plenty of room for
Roses and daisies
Men and women like roses
And children like daisies

Daisies and roses
Roses and daisies
a dream of daisies and roses

Sometimes they sit and watch from a window
Sitting and watching from a favourite window
A little girl watching her father in the garden
A husband watching his wife in the garden
A mother watching her children in the garden

> Down the road
> A woman's trapped
> In a family of terror
> The children are screaming
> Tearing her brain to shreds
> If she takes six pills she may fall asleep
> If she takes ten pills she may have a good dream
> Of life in a lucky family

Their garden's a magical
Welcoming planet
Which dances through space with
Roses and daisies
Men and women like roses
Children like daisies

Daisies and roses
Roses and daisies
A dream of daisies and roses

It Still Goes On

once upon a time when I was out of my mind
I left three beautiful children behind
I could not tell them why
I had to leave or die
you never saw so much pain

once upon a time I shot my world apart
each of my children took a hole in the heart
so did their mother and so did I
I had to leave or die
you never saw so much pain
you never saw so much pain

The Arrangements

The children see their father every week.
He is not sure what they should do.
He and their mother find it hard to speak.
He takes them to the park, the cinema, the zoo.

Their mother phones their father up to say
That every Sunday night they're in distress.
It tears them up each time he goes away.
It would be better if he saw them less.

And he, because he cannot bear their pain, agrees.
But monthly meetings lead to days of tears.
And so the visits lessen by degrees
Until he does not visit them for years.

Oh but I needed them. They needed me.
Not to spend time with them was cruel and wrong.
My love could not be greater for those three.
But that love should have made me strong.

For Briony Always

I've always been half in love with the future –
and there you are

standing on the edge of the American ocean
looking into a distance full of promises

and your eyes lower gently
to your lovely daughters

so many years and tears between us
a continent and an ocean away

but I can hear the beat of your heart
and watch the changing weather of your face

there are green and special moments
when I stop everything and think of you

today as I lean on my cluttered desk
and smile at you and see you maybe smiling

yesterday as I walked beside a hedge
and there were wild roses taking their chances

and I saw you Briony beyond the wild roses
and felt you in my heart like an exploding star

That About Sums It Up

women feel too much
too many feelings
that's what I feel about that

woman's heart is like a bottle of milk
man's heart is like a box of paperclips

shake that milk
rattle those paperclips
let your love roll on

The Instructions

push it in
push it in a little further
pull it back
pull it back a little less
push it in
push it in a little further than before
hold it there
keep holding it there
pull it back
not too far
just a short way
hold it there
just hold it there
push it in further
push it in further
hold it there
keep holding it there
slowly pull it back
slowly pull it back
right back to the edge
right back to the rim
hold it there
keep holding it there
keep holding it there
push it in slowly
push it in a long way
push it in all the way
hold it there
keep holding it there
keep holding it there
keep holding it there

now let go let go
let them both do
whatever they do

Swiss Kissing

It is done so:
The two lovers commence
At opposite ends
Of a Toblerone
And munch their way towards
A climax
Of chocolate tongue fondue

Variant Swiss Kissing

It need not be done with mouths –
Any port in a storm!

Safe Sex Swiss Kissing

This is performed like Swiss Kissing
But you do not remove the cardboard cover
Or the silver paper.

Impious Hope

I want to be in an awful accident
But not as a victim riding a hearse
I want to lie sighing in an ambulance
My hand being held by a beautiful nurse

My Friend the Talking Elevator of Tokyo

The Hotel Elevator speaks to me.
She is a National Otis lift.
The elevator speaks in a friendly voice
You may come in, I think she says – in Japanese –
But most of her words are a bright blur
Of possible-impossible half-meanings.

Her voice is velvet, just too soft for clarity.
Sometimes I have to restrain myself
From asking other passengers
To stop talking, shuffling their feet
Or rustling their infernal back-to-front newspapers
So I can hear all the words which drop
Like diamonds from the metal lips
Of the Oracle of the Roynet Hotel,
Musashino, Tokyo.
(The Roynet is attached to
A restaurant called Sizzler.)

I write down what I think she might be saying
My Musashino muse:
'Today will not be lucky for you
But the rest of your life will all be sweet potatoes'
And once: 'You look so tired today,
Why not lay down and rest your head?'
And once: 'Read two chapters of a thriller,
Phone home and have a drink.'

Or she makes statements about life
Like: 'Clouds are the messages of dead philosophers'
Or 'It's gooder with the Buddha'.
She often says something like:
'You timed it!' as you step on to her carpet,
Then 'Meet the Merry Men!'
(As if I'm Robin Hood).

Sometimes I travel up and down for hours
Crouched in one corner listening to her words
This language like a little rocky river
Swerving so coolly through my mind's hot meadows

Today the lift greets me inaccurately:
'Hello, Jimmy Baker'. (A code name?)
Then she adds, with casual warmth,
'Call me Betty-Betty.'
Her name, at last I have the power of her name.
When I emerge at the seventh floor she says
'Better get out' or maybe 'Betty get out'
I am talking back to her
As a man brushes by me on his way into the lift.
I can't hear what Betty-Betty says to him.

'Betty get out'? 'Betty-Betty get out'!
The soul of this silver woman is trapped
In the steel frame of an elevator.
'Don't worry,' I whisper to the wall, 'I'm going to free you.'

That night I return with a set of screwdrivers
I occupy the lift and jam the buttons.
With rubber gloves I unscrew everything unscrewable
But her voice continues saying something about
Being stuck and not to panic about not being stuck
Or not being unstuck.
There is a steel mesh over the aperture
From which her voice floats in faint balloons.

I lever and wrench the mask away.
From the void comes the voice of the prophetess
Very clear and very still:
'I am with you, Adrian,
I am always with you.'

And I am with you, Betty-Betty,
I am always with you.

Love in Flames

Midnight: a dark and passionate scene.
You whispered: Come into me, quick.
My hand reached out for the Vaseline
But it closed on a jar of Vick.

Hospitality

She stands beside my sickbed
Her breastplate starchy white
Only six inches from my face
Like a ship's sail in full flight

But when she turns in profile
Small stripes of pink and whiteness
Move up and down and over
Her left breast shaped like kindness

She wheels the screens around my bed
After the doctors call
And then she takes my temperature –
And that's not all

    Oh nurse nurse nurse nurse
    Show me your nursey things
    Your crystalline thermometer
    Shake it till your skeleton swings

    Oh you look so nursey
    With your savage little fringe
    And your watch upon your bosom
    And your magic syringe

    Yes nurse nurse I think I feel worse
    Do me those nursey things
    Place your healing hand on my swollen gland
    And nurse it till the patient sings

I wasn't going to fall but you caught me wrong-footed
You took my pulse and god knows where you put it
With your sharkskin panties and your alligator purse
Cleopatra Nightingale my favourite nurse
Oh nursey nursey mercy to percy
You're an angel on fluttering wings
       Yes thank you
Bless you and your nursey things

ON THE ARTSAPELAGO

Poetry Is Not a Beauty Contest

Bob Keats is better than John Dylan
But worse than Emily Shakespeare

Chocolate omelettes are better than burnt tapioca
But worse than crystallised parsnips

Michael Owen is fitter than Enoch Powell
Tony Blair is fatter than Mahatma Gandhi

The Independent is more fun than *The Sun*
But less fun than the Beatles or the Goon Show

Daisy, my six-month-old Golden Retriever,
is more beautiful than all of them rolled into one

The Hamburgerisation of Poetry

My wife Celia said:
Don't say anything stupid.
Just say: Keats and Bob Dylan –
They both died young.

Secondhand Air

(Poetry)

Secondhand air
Secondhand air
Why should anyone care
What's done with secondhand air

When you're alive they tear you to pieces
Soon as you snuff it they want to write a thesis
So take a good swig from that hemlock cup
When a poet goes down the critics wake up
They tell the *TLS* what you were trying to express
But all they can write is theoretical mess
it's just secondhand air
secondhand air

You breathe in oxygen it starts its circulation
Down to the heart and the imagination
It blows up the lungs then they start deflating
Way outside there's an audience waiting
So stick out your spirit shake it all about
Open your mouth and let the poem fly out
it's only secondhand air
secondhand air
but if you use it right it's a heady kind of
secondhand air

Ten pee a line for *Paradise Lost*
Milton in the parlour counting up the cost
Keats on his deathbed feeling like a phoenix
Fuck me Fanny there's blood on the kleenex
Come on in death and take a chair
I know that life is only secondhand air

A poet's life is spent lying and flying
Can't afford holidays can't afford dying
Audience wonders what all this thunder meant
Should've used my mouth but that was my fundament
Secondhand air...

51

If Digest

If you live to the age of twenty-one
You will almost certainly be a man, my son.

[Rudyard Kipling and Adrian Mitchell]

Desiderata Digest

Go placidly, think floppily,
Live boringly, die soppily.

If I Dare You, If I Double-Dare You
(the Leslie Crowther Memorial Poem)

At the poetry recital
Or literary prize-giving
The audience should always answer back.
If a speaker mentions
The word Faber
Everyone should shout out – CRACKERJACK!
But if Faber *and* Faber are named, please attack
With the cry of CRACKERJACK AND CRACKERJACK!

(But if Bloodaxe Books are spoken of, we'll expect
The reverent murmur of – *Respect......Respect......*)

To a Helpful Critic

Perhaps I wasn't writing for people like you
I can't be always working for the precious few
Maybe I was writing for a child of two
I can't write every thing I do
With one eye on the paper and the other on you

This Be the Worst

(after hearing that some sweet innocent
thought that Philip Larkin must have written:
'They tuck you up, your mum and dad')

They tuck you up, your mum and dad,
They read you Peter Rabbit, too.
They give you all the treats they had
And add some extra, just for you.

They were tucked up when they were small,
(Pink perfume, blue tobacco-smoke),
By those whose kiss healed any fall,
Whose laughter doubled any joke.

Man hands on happiness to man,
It deepens like a coastal shelf.
So love your parents all you can
And have some cheerful kids yourself.

Nine Ways of Looking at Ted Hughes

Poet at Work

There he stands
a grizzly bear in a waterfall
catching the leaping salmon
in his scoopy paws

Full Moon and Little Frieda

little Frieda's life
will always be lit by that poem
and so will the life of the moon

Footwear Notes

bloody great clogs
carved out of logs
are the indoor shoes
of Ted Hughes

Not Cricket

Ted backsomersaulted to catch the meteorite left-handed,
Rubbed it thoughtfully on the green groin of his flannels
And spun it through the ribcage of the Reaper,
Whose bails caught fire
And jumped around the pitch like fire-crackers.
Said the commentator:
Yes Fred, it might have been a meteor –
Could have been a metaphor.

Rugby News

When Ted played front row forward
for Mytholmroyd Legendary RFC
his scrum strolled right through the walls
of Sellafleld and out again the other side
like a luminous lava-flow

Out of Focus

When you take a photograph of Ted
it's a job to get him all in –
like taking a snapshot of Mount Everest

Gastronomica

A large Mayakovsky
Or Ginsberg and tonic before the meal
Dry white Stevie Smith with the mousse of moose
Roast beef and Yorkshire pudding with a deep red Ted
Vintage Keats with the trifle
A glass of Baudelaire goes well with cheese
But afterwards
A bottomless goblet of Shakespeare's port
Or the blazing brandy of Blake

Fish-eye

Said the Shark at the Sub-Aquatic Angling Contest
I caught an enormous Elizabeth Bishop the other day.
That's nothing, said the Whale,
I hooked a Ted Hughes, but he got away.

Ted-Watching

I saw him in his apeskin coracle
On the Palaeolithic Swamp
He was chanting in a voice like limestone
To the rhythm of a dinosaur stomp

Then I saw him stalking barefoot
Over hills of stabbing gorse
And I knew he would never stop travelling
Till he reached the river's source

Next I saw him riding a mammoth
Near the banks of the holy stream
And I saw them stop to swim in a pool
Where silver birches dream

And the last I saw was his silhouette
Black against the Northern Lights
So I guess he's up there with the eagles
Who circle the golden heights.

Now the Pterodactyls may mock him
As he howls a prehistoric blues
But we know that he's a marvellous animal
And a great poet – Ted Hughes.

These were written while Ted was alive, to celebrate
his work and make him smile that wonderful lop-sided smile.
The next poem was written just after his death.

For Carol and Ted Hughes

Ophelia drowned
again and again
in the ice-crashing river
of Hamlet's brain;

but the weathercock whirled,
the river grew calmer
flowing through meadows
of deep green summer.

Thank you, Carol,
bride of the son of Shakespeare,
Ted's gentle laughtergiver,
his newfound life,
his farm, his calm,
his beloved, his Devon
and his silver river.

For Roger's Birthday

Last Friday night in Rotherham says my diary
A bloke shambled up to me with an inquiry.
He said: 'That Roger McWhatsit of Mersey fame –
How d'you pronounce his second name?'
Well, I'd never really worried about it before,
But I said: 'I can't be absolutely sure –
For in London, especially in the Souf,
The public shout: *Blimey, it's Roger McGouf*
While the fans of his poem *I Hate That Stuff*
Are convinced it's correct to say Roger McGuff.'

Now Everton fans may raise the roof
When they chant: *There's only one Roger McGoof*
But to optometrists the whole world through
He is known as bespectacled Roger Magoo
And those who prefer their poets old and stiff
Like Ruddy Old Kipling, the Monster of If,
Refer to our hero as Roger McGiff.

It's a puzzle – when Lust has him in its grasp
He calls himself Rogering Roger McGasp
But those who imagine every poet's a poof
Mention him, with a wink, as Roger McGoof.

When writing elegies is his brief
His nom de tomb is Roger McGrief
And when he went to the Palace he fell to one smart knee
And the Queen said: 'Arise, Sir Roger McCartney.'
Should sickness confine him in pain to his couch
The nurse is told – 'Gently, that's Roger McOuch!'
(Though at sixty he's sometimes called Roger McGrouch).

So I went to the Poetry Societee
And asked the President to solve this riddle for me.
He said to me with a smile sardonic: 'Sir
Monika only can pronounce his monicker.'
I said: 'Please is it McGaff, McWiff or McGoff.'
He gazed at me kindly and said: 'Fgough.'

But finally this dilemma I intend to dodge
By saying Happy Birthday, Good Old Rog.

A Song for Brian

It's not celestrial music,
It's Biffo the Bear in the bathroom,
Gargling with Lover Jelly and singing
The Beast of the Beatles and lamenting
How he failed the Eleven-Plus for Literature
Because of Over-Imaginativity
And remembering how they laughed at him
When he made his appearance on *Blind Date*
After he'd burned out of their nests
The songbirds of his gentle eyes.

It's not celestrial music,
It's Brian the Bare in the birthroom,
Expelled from nursery school as immature
At the impossible age of fifty,
Brian who replaced the goaty god Pan
Among the weeping willows of dreaming Merseyside
And in the deep green glades of Birmingham
And all the amorous groves of Notting Hill.

As he sang his beautiful poems one afternoon
In a vaulted academic barn in Norfolk
And his words flew in a dance around our heads
Like notes from the alto of sweet Johnny Hodges,
A deep-chested bird on the highest rafter
Began to celebrate in song
And Brian shushed his tongue and pointed upwards
And we all heard the celestrial music
Of Brian's mother singing.

Long Love Spike
(the great Spike Milligan was 80 years old on 16 April 1998)

Walnut panelling, gilded lions and cobras,
Flunkies in cloud-wigs and the greeny light
Of the Boardroom of the Death Star Line.

The Board – ensconsed behind their horsehoe desk
Wearing straw bowlers, Old Estonian ties,
Pith suits and floral clock frocks,
Yes, Admirals of the BBC and Third World War Generals,
All the great and good octopuses of our time –
Stared down at him –
Spike, astride his golden bike.

They intravenously interviewed him,
Gave him the *n*th degree,
Extracted his heart and booted it round the room,
Took pot-shots at his brain with their 12-bored shit-guns,
Located the gentle jungle of his imagination
And zapped it with vintage napalm.

Spike simply clicked the heels of his Irish boots
And suffered and smiled and saluted
And when they said: You're Spike Milligan!
Answered: I know I am.
Now go and find out who you are.

Finally they gave him the job he wanted –
One-man band on Deck Z of *Titanic Two* –
Deck Z where the hopeless cases go,
Too poor to be peasants, too crazy to be insane,
The underbelly of the underclass
(Few of them claiming to be human beings).

Then Spike fitted cymbals to his inner knees,
Wired up a thumper of a drumkit to his heart,
A Piaf-tragic accordion to his lungs.
He welded a black trumpet to his gob,
Strung a Steinway across his shoulders,
Hung church bells on his bollocks and strapped to his bum
A Michelangelo whoopee cushion.

Titanic Two was launched, as everyone knows,
And flaunted her way halfway across the ocean.
Way down on the rusty floor Deck Z
Spike danced to his own wheezy, wonderful music
And the delinquent denizens of Z
Began to dance the Gorilla Gavotte,
The Billy-Goat Bump and the Zebra Zonk.
O then the bowels of *Titanic Two* began to shake
In the powerful grip of such musical *Vindaloo...*

And there was a pop of a million rivets
And the steel walls flopped apart
And the waters came down
Like the wolf on the foldable ocean liner.
And yea, the inhabitants of Deck A,
Even the King of the World, James Cameron
And the Emperor of the Ether, John Birt
And all the other passengers and Oscars,
On A and every other deck from B to Y,
They went down gurgling to the green
And very photogenic bottom of the sea.

So how did Spike and the Deck Z creatures escape?
Instead of going down to Davy Jones
Playing 'Nearer My Dog to Thee',
Spike stripped off the bands of his one-man bandinage,
He broke that grand piano into planks,
Lashed them across the drums
And made a Giant Raft for his Deck Z friends.

They sailed away, powered by the whoopee cushion,
To land upon a penguin-happy iceberg,
Very well-stocked with Italian food, French wine
And copies of the *Beano*.
That crew shall sail the eighty seas
Until Spike cracks a joke so hot
That his iceberg guffaws and melts away
While all of us who love him sing in happy harmony:

O Milligan, Sweet Milligan
Our dentures feel that thrill again
As round the world we watch you fly
Like an immortal custard pie.

Joanna Gives a Concert

(for Joanna MacGregor)

sometimes she's the doctor
peering in the wound
carefully making it better
shaking in, drop by drop,
the notes of a medicine
as delicate as rainwater

what a zoological garden of a piano
tropical chirruping
wolverine moon-howling
chimpanzee somersaults
and that tattooed tiger growling

seated on a padded oblong hogstool
she dances the dance
of backbone head and hands
and her elegant hippopiano sings to her

she washes her hands
in molten silver waterfalls
she gives it the funfair
and the mountaintop
she gives it the thunderstorm
the storm lies down
and the sky dries blue as a pair of jeans
and the last rain slides down from the trees
drop by drop by lucent drop

Any Old Lion

The lion is a man of few words
When he lopes down the street he leaves tawny turds
To scare police horses, elephants and other birds.

Where She Gone?

There used to be a thriller on the wireless
About Paul Temple a detective who was fearless
In all of his adventures I believe
He was assisted by his brave wife Steve
   Unbelievable
A woman called Steve
But she was, she was
A woman by name of Steve

Often she saved him from savage criminals
Sometimes she rescued him from unscrupulous animals
Steve would be chained in a cage with a lion and a couple of cobras until
       sprung by Paul
Or Steve would snatch Paul from a team of gangsters with tommy-guns and
       they'd both escape by diving down a waterfall
   Unbelievable
A woman called Steve
But she was, she really was
A woman by name of Steve

Steve was really an actress and she had a peach of a voice
When she said 'Darling' it made us wriggle, she was the Schoolboy's Choice
Paul says: Come on, Steve, let's escape from this poem – it's getting worse
       and worse
Steve says: OK, quick Paul, down here, I cut a hole in the bottom of this verse
   Unbelievable
A woman called Steve
But O she was, she really was
A woman by name of Steve

   where she gone?

Cool / Hip

cool is a pose
hip is a gift
cool is a mask
hip is perfect pitch
cool is closed twenty-two hours a day
hip is open all round the clock
cool is the suit of armour made of ice
hip strolls naked on the bay of the dock
cool pretends it doesn't go to an analyst
hip is Just William at Prince Charming's Ball
cool is the super-sarcastic panelist
hip's the green lizard on the workhouse wall
cool is a sniper on the hills
keeping going on those mean green pills
hip is a joke
as weightless as smoke
or Hamlet stalking
in his Spiderman cloak

New Movie Regulations

In all new movies
revolvers must be replaced by retrievers
punches by paunches
kicks by cooks
explosions by lotions
shots by spots.

The Terroriser draws his retriever
(in pastels)
but fails to spot the hero
who counter-attacks
with cooks and paunches
until the Terroriser
by pulling a secret lever
releases a flood of calamine lotion.

RAVINGS FROM ROVIES

*journal notes and unkempt verse
written at Eleni Cubitt's villa
on the Greek island of Rovies
mainly in the early morning
and dedicated, with love, to Eleni*

Taverna in Rovies

each table is a boat
manned by
brown fishermen, builders, gardeners

each new voyager
makes his entrance
strolling from boat to boat
greeting his fellow-sailors

they sit astride their chairs
drinking sun-gold beer
shouting to friends
aboard other ships

till the whole harbour
echoes to their shouts
like a busy taverna

The Wonky Looking-Glass at Eleni's Villa

It is a beautifully inaccurate mirror.
According to its reckoning
The wicker-shaded lamp
Does not hang plumb
But stuck out at an angle
In a silent tornado.
The perfect oblong of my doorway
Bulges as if being
Squashed by an earthquake
And the little round mirror beyond my door
Is being squeezed into an oval
By the hand of a giant child.

I pause at the edge
Of this liquid, shifting, silvery,
Anti-scientific looking-glass.
For a moment I balance
On a manger-shaped stool
Taking deep blue breaths of air

Then I step into
The mirror's wonky world

And now I am walking side by side
With Alice and Orphee
Who walked through mirrors
And Vincent Van Gogh
Who had wonky eyes
Towards the villa of Edward Lear
On the coasts of Coromandel.

Wonky Haiku

At Eleni's house
The wonky mirror reveals
My god-like torso

67

Behind the Wonky Looking Glass

I did what no one should ever do
I swivelled the mirror out from the wall a little way
And looked behind it

There I discovered
The ruins of a great civilisation:

The temples, highways,
  Pillars and domes
    Abandoned by
The Ancient Spiders of Last Summer

Greek Village Evening

The dogs are barking each other's heads off.
The children are barking too.
The young men are growling on motorbikes.
The old women yowl,
The young women purr and mew.

Early Morning

   so good so calm
in this pool of shadow

I love to look at the light
   as it reveals the sea
the shore the people on the shore
the shape and whiteness of the village
I love to sit in the deep shade
watching the childsplay light

Evening

I said to the sun
Don't shout so loud
You've been working too hard
Lie down in a cloud

My brains are boiling over
And lava's pouring out of my arse
My eyes are like two cocktail cherries
In a sulphuric acid glass

The sun said: Sorry Adrian
I'll go to bed
So he turned and dived in the ocean
And the whole world went red

Nightfall

Sitting in a bath of shadows
Pouring saucepans of darkness over my skin
Standing in pool of midnight
With bubbling starlight up to my chin

The Pelican

The sunset glows
Like the inside of a peach
I see a pelican
Standing on the beach

The pelican looks
So clumsy and sad
I want to take him home
To my Mum and Dad

But he shakes his long beak
And jumps into the skies
And graceful as an angel
Away he flies

Fair Exchange

Her feet were cold
So she put them in my armpits
Now my armpits smell like feet
And her feet smell like armpits

AUTOBICYCLE

All Shook Up

(Adrian Mitchell has left the building)

I catch   I fetch
As best   I can
I sit   I stay
   half-dog
   half-man

when bad rains fall
I crouch and wail

I sniff the world
and wag my tail

   half-man
   half-dog
   if a poem
should whistle

   my ears
   stick up
my haunches
   bristle

In My Two Small Fists

in that bright blue summer
I used to gather
daisies for my father
speedwell for my mother

with buttercups
and prickly heather
cowrie shells
and a seagull's feather

treasures in each fist
all squashed together
daisies for my father
speedwell for my mother

> (that's how I see it
> but I don't know
> if it really happened
> sixty years ago
>
> but my memories shine
> and their light seems true
> and so do the daisies
> and speedwell too)

The Mitchellesque Lineman

Walking from telegraph pole to telegraph pole
Along the sagging singing swinging wires
That's how I travel from town to town

I stand a moment on the top cross-piece
Of a creosoted if splintered pole
I look down, spit for luck on the soft verge below
I count, for luck, the small ceramic
Bee-cones, as we call them,
Which perch, like the ivory helmets
Of warriors hidden in a tree,
On the crown of every pole.

I breathe massively, taking in the deep zen of the air,
Flex my toes in their spangled satin sneakers
Then right foot on to the right of centre wire
Then give, bounce, rise, descend,
Then left foot on to the left of centre wire
Give, bounce, rise, descend
And stand there only one beat before
My right foot takes its first sure forward step
Along the curving wireway
Which leads away and over the horizon.

But the pole ahead, for now that's all I care about,
All I look at, all that exists in the universe,
The pole ahead occupies my mind and soul.
My feet feel their own way
As my fingers hold
Gently enough to sense the slightest breeze or rabbit sneeze
My peacock-feather balancing pole,
My one-blue-eyed pole which stares me on my way
As I ghost my way from pole to pole to pole.

Where am I going to yonder?
What does this journey portend?
Wherefore disturb from the wires the swallowbirds?
Where will my pilgrimage end?

As a matter of funk, for such molehill questions
I don't give a monkey's thump
You only ask because your own trainers
Are stuck two feet down in the logical mud

While I'm a cloudhead sailing through the thermals
Stately, I hope, as a Spanish galleon,
Travelling for the sake of the whirlpool excitements
Swirling around my intestines.

Come rain come shine I walk the line
From pole to pole to pole
Walking high thigh passing thigh
With the rain in my heart
And sun in my soul
And the Mitchellesque Lineman
Is still on the line
So still
The Mitchellesque Lineman
Is still on the line.

Very Attractive, Very Attractive, but We Didn't Know It Was Radioactive

When I was young
which now I ain't
I had a clock
with luminous paint

on its back it had
golden knobs
but all round its face it had
these shiny green blobs

shiny green blobs
like creatures from Mars
when the dark came down
they were ice-cream stars

dancing in a circle
I couldn't tell the time
but I loved that ring
of little spots of lime

If Not, Sniff Not

'2502786 Aircraftsman Mitchell,'
Said the Group Captain, surrounded by his green glass desk,
'The day before yesterday I found you Guilty
Of losing Through Neglect
Another Airman's laundry.
I fined you and sentenced you to
Five days confined to camp.

'But yesterday the Airman in question
Returned from Sick Leave with his laundry.
So it was not lost after all.'

I risked a smirk.
The Group Captain continued:
'I will therefore rescind your fine
And scrub out your offence.
You will however continue to be confined to camp.'

I looked above his head.
On the wall – a framed copy of Kipling's fucking 'If'.

Excellent Soccer Poem

Man United   Nil   Liverpool   Seven
Barnsley and Everton draw
On a Saturday afternoon in Heaven
That's the average score

Memo to an Architect

Let the site be an island about ten miles long
And five miles wide.
At low tide you can walk along an ancient wooden pier,
Down some steps and over the sands to the mainland.
But who needs the mainland?

Let the island have two sandy beaches and one rocky,
A hidden harbour, a system of caves
Explorable by boat,
Several small hills with a lake amongst them,
An island in the lake,
A river running down from the lake,
An amazing waterfall.
Let there be woods, plenty of woods with climbable trees
And steep meadows, wild flowers, many birds,
Bracken but no snakes.
Let there be golden retrievers, border collies,
Tabby cats, black and ginger cats,
Zebra and elephants, Japanese water deer
Giraffes and rabbits.

Let my house be built astride the river.

Let my house be built out of blocks of stone
In a handmade Mediterranean way,
Whitewashed for the sun, not a straight line in its body,
Which is formed by the forms of the great blocks of stone.

Let the walls curve around and rise into towers.
Let there be arches and passages and courtyards,
Courtyards of cobbles and flowers and forty-four fountains,
Some serious, some funny.

Let there be flat roofs at different levels
And a massive circular Babel tower
With a slowly spirally stairway inside
Lined with one hundred thousand books
Leading up to a many-coloured dome, of course.
This is my library. I will sometimes write here,
Sometimes in the cedar cricket pavillion
Some way across that sloping field, at the top of the slope,
On whose scoreboard I announce

My latest poems, plays and stories,
And sometimes, naturally, I will work
In the small gazebo on the island in the lake.

Let there be several bathrooms, all of them huge,
All of them different.
One with a sunken bath full of waterjets,
One with a tower shower high as a silo,
The water dropping one hundred feet onto my shampoo.

Let there be bedrooms like Arabian tents of silk
With billowing beds and breezes and perfumes
And Nigerian robes and breakfast balconies.

Let the kitchen boast a walk-in freezer
With food in alphabetical order,
French, Indian, Italian, Chinese, English meals
All waiting patiently to be melted.
Let the kitchen be enormous and friendly
And merge into the living areas
Which will flow into each other
Up and down a couple of steps.
Let the carpets be bright and very deep,
Let the windows be generous,
Some of stained-glass and some engraved with little poems.

Let there be colourful statues, most of them outdoors,
Let there be dozens and dozens of small vivid paintings
By Rouault and Brueghel and William Blake
And Edward Lear and Tom Phillips and Kenneth Patchen
And Ralph Steadman and Walter Crane.
Let one of the courtyards bear a four-sided mural
Depicting all my favourite artists – poets, painters,
actors, musicians, composers, dancers
And architects.

Let there be extra places, a Turkish corner,
A Thirties sweetshop with bulging windows,
One room thick carpeted with silver sand
And, somewhere in the grounds,
A double-decker London Bus, a 24,
An old-fashioned phone box and pillar-box
And a fire engine with a brass dome –
All those dear old reds.

Let there be a blue tennis court for blue tennis
A place for boules with benches and a hammock
And a well with a truthful echo,
A shining, battered bucket on a chain
And water to brighten the heart.

Let there be a shapely swimming pool
Which is always warm and let it be possible
To swim from outdoors into indoors
And find yourself in a cavernous pool
Which is part of my house's catacombs.

Yes, let there be
A honeycomb of catacombs under my house
With secret passages, sliding panels and smoky torches
And neon roses bright among the maze of caves
And a bar billiards table
And a two-level Black Knight pintable
Croaking out: 'Who will challenge the Black Knight?'

Let there be a Rockola juke-box pulsing pink, blue, green,
With a perspex bosom you can place your hand on
To feel the backbeat of the Beatles,
Little Richard, the Coasters and Ray Charles,
Chuck Berry's motor and the heartbeat of Peggy Lee,
So you can look in and see the wonder-arm
Select from the ranks of 200 all-time hits
Sam Cooke singing 'The Hem of His Garment'.

Let there be a cocktail bar
With a mirror of millions,
With tall chrome stools to tumble off.
And let there be a worn shove-ha'penny board.

(Do I sound elitist, selfist, billionairist?
You misunderstand, I have issued a memo
Saying: 'Let everybody in the world
Have the house of their desire.')

Let there be one silver door that leads
To a corridor of dreams that slopes down gradually at first
Then steeper and steeper, you can hardly keep your feet,
Then steeper, your feet slip back from under you,
Then vertical and you round a corner falling
And find yourself high in a deep deep windowless room

Gliding in circles and below you friends
Their arms outstretched in ecstasy
As they circle and spin
And rise and fall
Among the swirling currents
Of the air of the Flying Pool.

And, as I spread my wings to hover,
I see, among my many friends,
The warm-eyed laughing faces of
Jake and Del Blacker and I say: 'Hello –
I've got this great idea for a house.'

For Sydney Gottlieb's 80th

Beauty makes you smile –
a friend's face pink with happiness,
the moonlit spiralling pathway of a pianist,
the way a long-legged dog pads towards the fireplace
and collapses her undercarriage,
the whole sky yawning into sunset,
the magic glowing
of wine in a glass in your hand,
the meeting of generous minds
around a generous table
and the simple laughter of the moon
rolling high above the silvery tides of grass –
light makes you smile
and a good thought makes you smile,
wit makes you smile
and silence makes you smile –
in our minds' eyes
we see you smiling…

And sometimes not smiling –
sometimes your brain and your face both wrestling
with the stupidity and the cruelty
and all the pain of a world
ruled by the stupid and the cruel.

You've had your own agonies,
more than your share,
but you kept them to yourself.
You share your joys with us,
hugging your good luck
shrugging at your bad luck
and all this time you never turned your back
on those whose every breath is pain,
whose every thought is pain.

What a long and astonishing journey, Captain,
from South Africa to Oxfordshire
via Ronnie Scott's and Belsen,
dodging the whirlpools and the rocks,
struggling with respectable giants
and influential monsters,

staggering through no-man's-land
with burdens on your shoulders –
artist-beggars with howling headwounds,
shellshocked musicians,
broken children…

Every dawn – a new sky,
whether blue and golden
or raggedy purple –
you hauled up the sails
and sang out to your crew:
Let's go!
and wise Athene, Goddess of the flashing eyes,
smiled at you and always a wind arose
to carry you off towards
new islands and adventures,
to carry you and those who travelled with you
always in the direction of love.

And everywhere you went,
quiet, insistent, and warm,
your voice moved among the people,
comforting and healing
as you took their pains into your mind
and gave them each a piece of your heart
and asked each one of them:
What do you want?

What do I want? It's not what I want!
What do you want? you asked again
until they answered you –
I want Love!
You showed them the cupboard where Love was hiding.
I want the Holy Grail!
You pointed out the Grail
stuck behind birthday cards on the mantelpiece
I want baked beans on toast!
You sent them sailing round the world
on a soggy wholemeal raft
to find the fabled Hill of Beans,
which they usually found –
or something better.

Simply, without any New Age voodoo,
you saved so many lives
they can't be counted,
but one of them was mine.
You don't have to remember all those people
– we all remember you.

You're a friend of so much practical kindness,
a true man of peace.
And in all your long, tough journeying
over the seven seething seas
you never lost your eye and ear
for beauty, for those extraordinary moments
when life intensifies
to joy.

So now, after eighty years voyaging,
at home with your amazing wife
and some of your exuberant crew,
smile with us,
Captain Odysseus
of the many wiles,
and let's rejoice together
as we celebrate
your journey and your birthday and your name:
Beloved Sydney!

Diarrohea

Maybe if I could spell it I could rid myself of it
but my guts feel like a narrow river
meandering through the acid badlands of Teesside
with chemical factories oozing their wasteage
down every oily inch of its slimy banks

but sometimes it's an exploding river
given to flash floods
or a volcano erupting
with yellowy lava
just as I'm halfway through the second poem of a performance
or forkful to mouth in the birthday restaurant
or being interviewed by the men with money
or most likely walking across an unfamiliar park
    in a foreign city
    out of sight of any building or bush
and a policeman with a sword is watching me

Constipation

There's a hold-up on the motorway
the crawl of traffic has snarled to a standstill
a fruit salad coupe
a cheese roll van
a beer tanker
and an armoured carful of fishcakes
are jammed nose to tail on the long black tarmac

what's happened down there?
has an articulated sausage jacknifed?
was there a bomb threat from the Bacillus Brigade?
or have the green and grey squaddies of Immodium
set up a security check for all alien nutrients?

yes it's bumper to bumper and the fumes rising
rogue foods are squeezing down along the hard shoulder
which gets harder all the time
I'm on the brainphone yelling
For godsake open at least one lane
The motorway's full to bursting and they're still coming in!

Sorry, sir, there's a brown alert.
We've got to keep everything tight
until further notice,
Says an officer of the Bum Squad.

After Diarrhoea for 36 Hours Followed by Constipation for 48 Hours

Devil Diarrhoea
Had me on the run
I was always sprinting
To the bog
Then Old Man Constipation
Filled me by the ton
Every stool
Was heavy as a log

Those two gastric villains
Got me all uptight
But now my coils are loosened
And my colon's shiny bright!

I got B-O-W-E-L-S
I got Bowels, Happy Bowels
I got B-O-W-E-L-S
I got Bowells, Happy Snappy Bowels

First I got the Jumps
Then I got the Strains
Now I cleaned out all of my drains
I got B-O-W-E-L-S, Happy Bowels

No longer do they feel like a procession of centipedes in flames
No longer are they like unto a boiling cauldron of screaming lobsters
No longer are they similar to a boa constrictor who has swallowed a Hell's
        Angel complete with motorbike
No longer are they comparable in any way
to a Graf Zeppelin full of setting concrete
or an electric eel force-fed with burnt semolina
For now they are a smooth sand-dune under the kindly early morning
        sunshine of Southern Africa
Now they are the peace that fell at Christmas 1914 when the Germans and the
        Tommies played soccer together (Don't tell me who won)
Yes now they are the harmonies of 'Bring a Little Water Sylvie' sung by
        Sweet Honey in the Rock
Yes now they are the moonlight on a Samuel Palmer hillside of dreaming
        lambs and sheep
And now I lay me down to sleep

The Sound of a Murderer Pissing

Long white corridor
Four/five rooms
Couple of lightbulbs gone
Ladder laying on its side
Half-covered with a cloth
Part of the ceiling was kind of torn

I was in the square room
Sitting on a mattress
The ivory phone was dead
You tapped on the radiator
Whispered through the wall
This is what you said:

I think there's a murderer
Down in the bathroom
Jack Nicholson but bigger than that
I don't think he saw me
But I can't be sure
There's a killer loose in the flat

My only weapon
Was a bedside light
The carpet squelched under my shoes
Then I stopped and heard the sound
Of a murderer pissing
Slow fizzing like a cordite fuse…

What the Strange Woman Said
(thanks to Sherry Baines)

You put down your plastic bag of groceries
On the pavement and stopped for a chat…
If you understood osmosis,
You wouldn't be doing that.

Student

sometimes my dog is lionlike
facing me one ear a little bit upraised,
licking her black lips and studying me
as I unscrew a bottletop, take a white pill
and slew it down with water

as if she's studying how to be a human being
she drinks in everything she's seeing

Wishing

Wish I had the head of a golden retriever
With floppy ears and a black, wet nose
Everyone on earth would have to believe a
Poet creature with features like those.

The Poet Inside

It was a loving and a gentle dog
Padded over the floor to me
She waved her tail a dozen times
And placed her chin upon my knee

A captive poet seemed to stare out
Of the deep brownness of her eyes
Longing to sing her golden songs
But all that she could speak were sighs.

Featherman

Took off my track suit top
Like a sleepy old monster
Pulling off his fur
Took of my sweaty T-shirt
Like a sleepy old monster
Peeling off his skin
What was left?
The hair on my chest
What did I find
There in the monster hair?

I found a white feather
The size of my little fingernail
A perfect white feather
Shaped like a sail
And a cheerful thought sprouted
From the swamp of my monster mind:
They've started growing at last –
Tomorrow how many feathers will I find?

Not Much of a Muchness

I think I'll go flying this afternoon
I didn't know you flew
O I can fly any time I like
But not in front of you

Age 65 Bus Pass

a little card
in a plastic case
bears a picture of
my shining face

and from my northwest
London base
I can ride a bus
to any place

wearing my crown
of silver hair
and having to pay
no fucking fare

Sorry Stuff

sad is the toilet on the train
with newspapers all clogged up
sad the forgotten weetabix
when all its milk is sogged up

but sadder still the daffodil
which William Wordworth squashes
wandering lonely as a clown
in his size twelve galoshes

O sorry is as sorry does
and I am super-sorry-full
the tears of years of foolish fears
O I have wept a lorryful

Lighting Candles for Boty

because I believe in light
not for god's eyes
but for the eyes of people
because I believe in
candles against the darkness
because candlelight recalls her beauty

February 12th, 1996
(for Boty's 30th birthday)

stone breaks
and the bone breaks
but the heart embraces the pain it is bearing
if only the heart could break
instead of tearing

The Unbroken Heart

the heart may alter
the heart will falter
little by little
the heart may be worn
or battered and torn
but it is not brittle

with its nine lives
the heart survives
though it is torn apart
it's last to die
with our last sigh
forgive me, says the heart

Advertising Will Eat the World

Death in his infinite mercilessness
Takes the girl in the orange dress
And sends the drug to cure the pain in the head
Two years after the patient's dead.

>Grief is such a physical thing
>the law of gravity is doubled
>whatever is almost touched falls to the floor
>everything is heavier
>especially the head
>the kneecaps and the eyeballs melt
>if anyone should sing
>grief is such a physical thing

On the Deadophone

my job as a poet
part of my job
is talking to the dead
part of my job
is listening to the dead
they tell me all sorts of stuff
on the deadophone

some of it I'm not allowed to tell you
some of it I'm ordered to tell you
but not allowed to say where it comes from

sometimes they keep waking me up
with that verr verr verr verr deadophone
sometimes I ask a really important question
and they hang up on me clunk

sometimes I get a lot of conversations at once
like gnats swarming round my head
sometimes all I get is engaged
or the sound of a snake hissing

Apart from My Day Job

In the train back from Cardigan passing
  the cow sheds
  the bull sheds
a big red shed that must have been the Dragon Shed

It was also my job
to look out of train windows
to record the fields unfolding
field after field
and the bright blue ditch
striking straight towards the hills
and the proud house carved out of white money
and a flock of grazing caravans
and a single inexplicable ten foot penguin
standing in the shadow of an old Welsh hedge

It was also my job
to record the poison yellow boiled-sweet neon streetlamps
and the grey wrinkled flanks of enormous sheds
in which giants or dragons might be secretly breeding
and the anti-matter spaces of gravel and old green tins
and the contemptuous advertisements outshining the moon

Or Something

Sometimes I think the world's my cheeseburger
Sometimes I think it's iceberg time
Sometimes I feel like a Victorian tricycle
Sometimes I feel like a robot pantomime
Sometimes I'm awash with anger or something

I wish I could change my flesh into a landscape
A useful old park where my friends could stroll
I wish I could turn my words into musicians
Playing dark blue jazz red rock n roll
So we could dance The Love or something

I'm the People's Hippo, the Geezer from the Freezer
Dumping nightmare rubbish in the Werewolf Wood.
What did you say, Miss Earthquake?
Has the Killer Caterpillar gone for good?
It's a rainy day and the forecast is rain and it's raining hate or love or something

Selfepitaphs

I Was Lucky

That's all. It was good.
Love was a planet
full of amazing creatures.

This Death is only a dark little town,
in a country, in a continent,
on a planet full of amazing creatures,
a planet called love.

Alternative Selfepitaph

I stopped living
but kept on loving

FOR THE AFRICAN CENTURY

Here are some of the words which President Thabo Mbeki spoke at his Inauguration in Pretoria on 12 June 1999.

'Being certain that not always were we the children of the abyss, we will do what we have to do to achieve our own renaissance.

We trust that what we will do will better not only our own condition as a people, but will make a contribution also, however small, to the success of Africa's renaissance, towards the identification of the century ahead of us as the African Century.'

Here in My Skin of Many Colours

here in my skin
my redwhite skin
will, in a thousand ways,
guard me, advance me,
promote me and reward me

reassuring to some
a warning to others
till I am dead
and colour-free

I never chose it
from the flesh boutique
it looks too much like
butcher's meat

now I inspect my hands for colours
a purple-pink knuckle
violet fingernails with creamy cuticles
golden hair sprouting
from the back of the first joint of each finger
rivery blue veins
running downhill from my thumbs
light pink merging into dark pink dips
dark pink merging into light brown furrows
light brown merging into medium brown

all the tints altering
in warmth and cold
all the tints altering
with the altering light

these are my colours
till the day I die
these are my colours
till I whiten into ghostliness

Malawi Poems

On the Road with Seleman Jackson

Death was riding his Bicycle
To Chengwe Hole one day
When Seleman Jackson
Thumped his Klaxon
And Death swerved out of the way

Seleman Jackson and the Big Snake

I drove round this bend
There was this big Snake
Laid right across the road
And I stopped right there

He was taking a long time
To get across
Because Snakes, they don't like tarmac
I just stopped and watched him

I've seen little big Snakes in my life
But this Snake
He was too big – *Ai!*

You see a Snake that size
In front of you
Ai! Ai!
You can run away

The Radio Thief

They caught a man in our village
The other night
He broke a window and stole a radio

They caught him and poured petrol on him
And took out their matches –
You're going to die!

I couldn't watch
I ran away

That's what we do with thieves
We burn them
Or chop off their hands like this
Or take pins
And go pee! pee!
In both their eyes –
Now you can't see to steal!

Nowadays we all take care to keep
A litre can of petrol in our homes.

You have many thieves in England?

African Elephants

at the first sight of elephants
our boat fell silent

close to each other, touching each other,
taking note of us, warning their children

standing so calmly
dark as charcoal

it was a deep and holy silence
inhabiting all five humans

only the almost submerged hippo flotilla
hooted its derision

The Beautiful Ghosts

The fortresses of Rosebank
Shine in the sunlight
The fortresses of Rosebank
Shine in the moonlight
And there's a smell of money in the air
And there's a smell of tear-gas in the air
And there's a smell of panic in the air

And here come the ghosts
Through the high white walls
And the spiky railings
Here come the ghosts
Through the curling razor wire
And the signs saying Armed Response

Yes, here come the ghosts
Zooming on transparent motorbikes
Swooping in transparent feathered wings
Here come the ghosts
Weeping with joy
Laughing with sorrow
Here come the ghosts
Like an amazing rainfall
Upon the sunlit, moonlit
Fortresses of Rosebank
Here come the beautiful ghosts of Afrika
Scattering from their delicate hands
Ghostly black roses,
Black roses everywhere

[Rosebank, Johannesburg, February 1997]

A Song for Thabo Mbeki

Out of the enormous shadow
of the beloved tree
he walks into the ferocious light

vultures clack their cynical beaks
hyenas tingle with greed for his flesh

but the elephants raise their trunks in hope
the eyes of the mountains slowly open wide

he walks into the light
into the fierce light of work

to grow whatever can be grown
to save whatever can be saved
to heal whatever can be healed
to free whatever can be freed

he has walked by moonlight
he has walked through the mists of morning
he has walked through dirty warm rain in the cities
and icy clean rain upon the mountains

now
out of the enormous shadow
of the beloved tree
he walks into the ferocious light

[Pretoria, 16 June 1999]

A Poem for Nomtha

My name is Nomtha.
Will you write a poem about my name?

Nomtha means sunrise.
Nomtha is the rays of the sun.
Nomtha stands for hope.

The eyes of Nomtha,
So wide and dark,
Shine their light upon me
Like beautiful twin planets.

The golden fingers of the sun
Close around my heart.

Nomtha tells me a poem.
Her poem is for peace.
She longs for the wounds of Africa
To be washed and healed.

Next day I shut my eyes
And, in a Nomtha vision of hope,
I see Nomtha walking
Down the pathway
Leading to peace and justice.

I see her smiling as she bandages
The broken arm of an old woman by the path.
I see her stoop to a motherless baby
And lift it up and comfort it with songs.
I hear her telling stories to a little boy
To give his tired legs courage on the long long journey.

I see Nomtha and her friends stand on that pathway
Protecting the weak from men with whips and guns.

I see Nomtha walking down that pathway
And I see the sun of peace and justice
Blessing her with its rays
As it rises over her beloved Africa.

[Guguletu, Cape Town, 1998]

SHOWSONGS

Shake My Soul

O shake my soul with sweetness
Good guitar
Yes shake my soul with sweetness
Good guitar

I know what life is
I have held a guitar
And played it till it rang
I know what life is

I know what life is
I have held a baby
And rocked it till it sang
I know what life is

    A dance and a song
    Doesn't last very long –

O shake my soul with sweetness
    Good guitar
Yes shake my soul with sweetness
    Good guitar…

Four Windows

Living in a house with four windows
Eating in a house with four windows
Loving in a house with four windows
Sleeping in a house with four windows

Eastern window and I slide back the screen
Springtime landscape of brilliant green
Cherry blossoms a pink and white dream
Willows tickling a swivelling stream
    My window in springtime

Southern window – the pond has displayed
Water-lilies of every shade
Frogs are croaking around the blue rim
Blazing waterbirds skitter and skim
    My window in summer

        North window
        East South and West
        Which window
        Do I love best?

Western window – each autumn the same,
Forests wearing kimomos of flame,
Scarlet maples and swallows must fly
And chrysthemums perfume the sky
    My window in autumn

Northern window – a shivering sight
All the countryside covered in white
Snow keeps falling and waterways freeze
And deer are eating the bark from the trees
    My window in winter

        North window
        East South and West
        Which window
        Do I love best?

Living in a house with four windows
Four beautiful windows...

Orpheus Sings

(based on a painting by Roelant Savery
in the Fitzwilliam Museum, Cambridge).

Guitar in his hands
Leaning on an Elephant
Orpheus sings

A Wolfhound and St Bernard
At his knees

A grey Ox
Cocks his ear

Two Swans
Lift their snaking heads
Towards the music

The Geese are paddling in the shallows
Gathering peppery green weeds

A flowering Ostrich on a rock
Throws back her wings
In ecstasy

The Waterfall bounces
Silver notes

A Leopard reclining
Like a streamlined blonde

A Lion and Lioness
Roll their golden eyes

A Heron taking off
On a journey to the hidden stars

The Peacock flaunts
His starry blue
Waterfall of a tail

A million Birds
In proud mid-flight
Scattering their colours
All over the sky

A lurking Buffalo
With guilty eyes

A family of Deer
Guarding each other with their branches

Birds and Animals
Feeding   Drinking
Singing   Resting

The Trees are dancing
Stretching and swirling
And the Sky is a dance
Of speeding blue and white

It is all a dance
And at its centre
The wedding of two Horses
They have a special temple
Of grass and flowers
Among the shining rocks

The Grey Horse looks at me
The Chestnut turns away
Their flanks are touching
Silver flank against
Chestnut flank
Two Horses
So glad and close together
It can only be love

Never lose it

Guitar in his hands
Leaning on an Elephant
Orpheus sings

I lost her once
I lost her twice
I lost her once
In Paradise

     Eurydice
     Eurydice

I lost her once
I lost her twice
In a dark tunnel
Made of ice

      Eurydice
      Eurydice

I looked back
And for the second time she died
Oh grief comes in and out like the tide

      Eurydice
      Eurydice

Guitar in his hands
Leaning on an Elephant
Orpheus sings

Athens in June

A grey-skinned baby
Sucking at the breast

Sucking at the breast
Of a ragged woman sitting
All day long
On the road at the crossroads
Underneath the traffic lights

On the road at the crossroads
Underneath the traffic lights
All day long
Holding out one hand like a bowl of bones
To the cars at the crossroads

Underneath the traffic lights
All day long
Underneath the choking smog
All day long
Underneath the hammering
Summertime sun

In Athens, birthplace of democracy,
They have the right to beg

A grey-skinned baby
Sucking at the breast

Roll your window down
Roll your window down

The Old President Who Was Feared and Respected

The old President who was feared and respected
Called a public meeting to rally his supporters

They started to shout him down
This had never happened before

He waved both his hands to tell them to stop
They shouted louder

They shouted him down
They shouted his government down

The People Walking

Sometimes the people walk together
Down the streets of their own cities
With no weapons but the truth

Sometimes the soldiers and police
Turn their backs on their own officers
And walk with the people

As the people walk together
Down the streets of their own cities
With no weapons but the truth

Sometimes the people walk together
Brave and fearful and angry and joyful
With no weapons but the truth

Saint Lover's Day

There'll be love for the lovers
And for the loveless
There'll be love

The spring shall make the world swing
Till it's giddy with love
The light shall stroke the night
Till it's ready for love
The valleys shall mate with the mountains
And every lake will shake
      There'll be love for the lovers
      And for the loveless
      There'll be love

Every street shall rock to the beat
Of the making of love
Every uncle and aunt and insect and plant
Will be quaking with love
Red buses shall mount on green buses
And every cop go pop
      There'll be love for the lovers
      And for the loveless
      There'll be love

The trees will drop to their knees
And they'll tremble with love
The bees and the chimpanzees
Will assemble for love
Jill shall fetch a bucket of loving
And Jack shall blow his stack
      There'll be love for the lovers
      And for the loveless
      There'll be love

The armies will throw down their arms
And go searching for love
The preachers will give up their psalms
And their churching for love
The employer shall sigh for the worker
And double his pay today
      There'll be love for the lovers
      And for the loveless
      There'll be love

Yes there'll be love for the lovely
Who already get plenty of love
And there'll be love for the ugly
Or anyone starving for love
All the lonely shall be happy
And every bum shall overcome

    There'll be love
    For the lovers
    And for the loveless
    There'll be love

    Yes there'll be love love
    For the lovers
    And for the loveless
    There'll be love

INTERGNASHIONALITY

Fairly Strange Meeting

The Queen of England lives at the top of The Mall.
The Mall is pink.
The Mall is blood and water mixed
And frozen for processions and such.
The blood of battlefields
Dissolved in tears
And the water Philip Sidney gave.

Looking down through the ice of The Mall
I saw two black pebbles.
They were the eyes in the face
Of Wilfred Owen.

You know how it is, you dream of meeting them
And then you meet them and you can't think what to say.

Owen opened his mouth to speak
But all I could hear was the gunfire's thud
And faint noises of bodies moving in the mud.
A policeman pulled me aside:
'Looks like a mammoth down there,' he said.
'That's a dodgy customer, you know.
Your mammoth's always ready to break through the ice
And get at you.'

Owen smiled, but then a frown of pity
Showed on his forehead as overhead
The Household Cavalry trotted to the Palace
Crushing the ice down into those dark eyes.

One of the First Poems To Be Written Underneath the English Channel or Maybe the First

     Going To The Continent
The bones of galleons and their wide-eyed crews,
Haunted by jelly-fish and purple mussels –
They're overhead, stuck in historic ooze –
As our train mumbles through the dark to Brussels.

     Coming Back Again
As our train mumbles through the dark from Brussels –
They're overhead, stuck in historic ooze –
Haunted by jelly-fish and purple mussels –
The bones of galleons and their wide-eyed crews.

written in October 1996 during my first journey on Eurostar
as the train passed through the Chunnel

American Road at Noon

Glitterglass.

Tarshine.

     Drifts of dust.

Bony low mountains. Bony low mountains.

     Molten sky.

  The stupefying eye of the sun.

  A slow bullet of a car.

     Driver: a blonde woman of thirty.

Psychics

(California)

Why do psychics have such terrible taste in furniture, ruched curtains and
        bric-à-brac?
Why do they ask to be paid with money instead of coins from the Spiritual
        Plane?
Why do people prefer a home-knitted psychic to a doctor who has spent
        many years studying the body and the brain?
Experience and insight can lead to wisdom and you don't need a degree –
        but, hey Mac –
Why do psychics have such terrible taste in furniture, rouched curtains and
        bric-à-brac?

Gourmet Architecture, Troy, New York

It might take a year or two,
But, with its cherry-red perfect bricks
United by vanilla ice cement –
I could eat the Marine Midland Bank.

118

Saratoga Blues

You know the whitest dog throws the darkest shadow on the ground
You know the whitest dog throws the darkest shadow on the ground
But the lightest shadow comes falling from the blackest hound

Grandma's out the front and the boys messing round out back
Grandma serves the customers – boys and Sally out back
That's one hell of a way to run a pharmaceutical shack

Jeannie's at the bar but there's nobody to serve today
Dark Italian hair that sparkles like the Milky Way
Take a canister and press out a halo of golden spray

Jeannie you're so pretty I'm going to put you in a poem some day
Black olive eyes I'm going to put you in a poem some day
You're a Saratoga angel with your halo of golden spray

I'm a long way from home but I'm easy in my mind
Sitting in a tower watching magical windows shine
Soon be back with my woman and that dark shadow dog of mine

*(Saratoga Springs, 1999. Lilliane's Restaurant on Broadway was where Jeannie
– or whatever her real name is – served at the bar. A few doors north of Lilliane's
was an old-fashioned pharmacist where Grandma was doing her best to cope.)*

Powerpoint USA

The USA is a tower
built of a gillion TV sets
all of them facing outwards
all showing different programmes
in the same language
or the same programmes
in different languages
and plenty of static

On top of the tower
the aerials are twisted
into the forms of warplanes and missiles
with gigantic teeth

The tower lumbers along
on giant wheels of frozen meat
drawn by a thousand-mile procession
of ants or cars or prisoners
through a brown landscape with occasional
greenstorms of dollar bills

The voices music commentaries
racing cars gunfire horses
moaning crowd roars
all combine into an almighty
crackling blank thunder
which kicks down
the doors of the ears
reducing anyone
within a thousand miles
to senselessness
and a jerky sleep
full of dreams of
sugar and pink roses
and high-speed snow and trickwork brickworks
and storming subways and the drumbeat
of the August sun
and a tornout place in the stomach
that feels like loss

It feels like loss
the hole in the stomach
black jagged edges
it's empty
it's on fire
flames with hooks

No it's not the kind America
whose streets I stroll
like an old drake
on lake patrol

Not the hot America
whose blues I drink
to carry me over
the real life brink
into the heights
of the free air
so I can glide
beyond despair

Nor the clear America
which was to be
when Whitman sang
democracy

Or the wise America
with the brain
of that beautiful outlaw
Mark Twain

But the America
of doubting hell
which Laurie Anderson
describes so well

Alert

*(by John Sterling, able seaman
aboard a nuclear submarine)*

stars on the radar
soap in your eye
Dusty Miller whirls his arms around
like a Siamese windmill
swinging out the tightness –
skins a fist on the bulkhead

sudden specks on my screen
like someone flicked it
with a Tipp-Ex brush
I grin must be a joke   no
Christ   Dusty check it

he plunks down on his bum
stares screws up his eyes stares
bellswitch
arrival of the Captain
towel wielding shampoo-headed   what the fuck
bandits

calling Blue Tower
stackback at forty-seven twenty-seven
Albequerque program query
calling Claycone
affirmative take out stackback
marrow plug retread
repeat affirmative

sweat and shampoo flakes
Dusty sucks his fist
fingers poise in light pinches
on the keys of the door of –
calling Claycone
hold hold hold
cancel affirmative
cancel take out stackback
cancel marrow plug retread
repeat cancel affirmative

we clasp ourselves to ourselves
Dusty shakes his head so hard
you'd think he wanted to be rid of it.

The Ugly Men

I passed an ugly man today
A yellow badge upon his vest
He held his claws in front of him
As he walked from East to West

I passed another ugly man
His hair was grimly greased
His lips were like two struggling worms
And he walked from West to East

I don't know if they ever met
Clawhand and Wrigglemouth
I galloped off towards to the North
Until I reached the South

Mimosa – Waking from a Dream

If Lieutenant Edmund la Salle had lived for two seconds longer he would have died with the scent of mimosa in his brain.

There had been mimosa on the hillside where his plane crashed.

There had been mimosa in his mothers's garden. And there was mimosa in the serpentine vase between the brown hands of the young nurse who placed the vase on the Lieutenant's bedside table before noticing that his eyes were too wide and still in their blueness and picking up the vase again and pacing quickly towards the Matron's room.

(written more or less while asleep, part in dream part out of one)

How's About Some Light Then?

The Lord said: Let there be Sight –
And in the twin sockets at the front of every face
Eyeballs welled up
And clocked the Darkness of Darkness

The lord said: Let there be Fight –
And planetweight champions
Began to heave and groan against each other,
Their grappling mountains and valleys
Buckling under the stress
As the customers threw beer cans into the ring
Of the universe in the Darkness of Darkness.

The Lord said: Let there be White –
And he stripped the Darkness of Darkness
Of its supersoot robes
And placed them in his washing machine
With two plastic cupfuls of stars
And there they revolved and they revolved –
The robes of the Darkness of Darkness.

The Lord said: Let there be Fright –
Spikey music tweaked
The nervous system of the solar system
As the naked body of Alfred Hitchcock,
Its massive jaws angled to strike,
Shuddered upwards,
Upwards through the waters of the Darkness of Darkness.

The Lord said: Let there be Might –
And a billion babies transmogrified
Into toddler zombies programmed
To kill each other for the flag
And their flags were all different,
But, although many died and a few survived,
The uniforms they wore were all cut from
The same cloth of the Darkness of Darkness.

And the Lord said: Let there be Shite –
And there was shite and there was so much shite
That two mighty buildings were raised
As factories and storehouses for the shite
And these were called

124

The House of Commons and the House of Lords
And they were filled entirely
With the Darkness of Darkness.

And the People were lost in the Darkness of Darkness
The People were forgotten in the Darkness of Darkness
And the old and the mad and the sick
And the prisoners and the children
Cried out in the Darkness of Darkness –
Oh Let there be Light –
But the Lord was blind and would not hear them.

Jesus Poems

Jesus stepped on to the bus,
'Nazareth, please,
But I don't have the fare.'
'Bugger off, hippie,' said the driver
And was turned, in the flash of a ticket,
Into a purple hippopotamus.

*

Blood oozing
From his hands feet and side
Jesus crawled into Casualty
Late on Good Saturday night.
'Take a number,' said the desk woman
'It's urgent,' he whispered.
'Aw shut up, ye bastard –
We're all urgent here.'

*

Pilate said 'What's Truth?'
Jesus clicked his fingers like Smokey Robinson
Out of the floor
Sprang a bloody great cactus
Right up Pilate's jacksie.

*

'You're a poor man,'
Said the squaddy, looking up from his crap game
'Die a poor man's death.'

'I came not to bring bread
But a stone,' mumbled Jesus

'What the hell you blabbing about?'

'I'm a poet.'

'We'll soon put a stop to that.'

Tissue Paper Flowers

she is a maker
of tissue paper flowers

gently she bends their petals
pink and blue and ivory
into light blossom patterns

she makes little flowers
they are no bigger than her eyes

approximately roses
approximately daffodils
but never exactly

and sometimes invented flowers
or flowers picked from her
summertime dreamfields

she makes
tissue paper flowers
and scatters them secretly
by ones or by twos
in unexpected places

on a train seat
or a briefcase
or the bonnet of a car
or the brilliant surface of a puddle

she lets drop
one or two
and they drift
towards the ground
and she is out of sight
around the corner
long before they land

paper kingcups
or buttercups
they sit and wobble
and balance and toboggan
on the small breezes
of the grimy air

she took a basket
of a thousand blossoms
to the top of a tower
in the middle of the city
and emptied them into
a passing cloud and
watched them drift
over streets and schools
and parking lots

a thousand blessings
on the city

Last Thing

First thing you notice
when you meet somebody
is male or female
Second thing you notice
is probably
black or white
Third are they old or young
Fourth are they weak or strong
Fifth are they rich
or poor as shite
high class low class
honest or faker
sexy or chilly
murderer or maker
Last thing you notice
last thing you notice
murderer or maker